Through It All...

KEEP on PRAYING

~ A collection of Poems ~

Through It All...

KEEP on PRAYING

~ A collection of Poems ~

Dr. L. Venchael Booth

Copyright © 1997 by
Dr. Lavaughn Venchael Booth
P.O. Box 32319
Cincinnati, OH 45232

Scripture quotations are taken from the *Holy Bible,
King James Version*

Library of Congress Catalog Number: 97-094222

ISBN 0-9655514-2-3

Inspirational/ Poetry

Printed in the United States of America

Inspiring Word Publications
P.O. Box 42057
Cincinnati, OH 45242

Dedication

I dedicate this book

To: The loving memory of my parents:
Rev. Fredrick D. and Mamie Booth

To: Brothers: Lemuel D., Galen C.,
Sister: Wilmetta Boykin

To: Georgia M., (my deceased wife)
Our five children:
Lavaughn V., William D., Anna M.,
Georgia A., Paul M.
and most especially
My wife, Yvette L. Booth

Additionally

To: All the churches I have served
and loved during my long ministry.

With Sincere Gratitude,

L. Venchael Booth

Acknowledgments

Special thanks to Mrs. Bertha McMillian, who many years ago typed and bound my poems, thereby preserving them for publication.

Thanks also, to The Reverend H. Jean Marshall, for her consultation and the many hours she spent organizing this book.

A special word of thanks is expressed to Mr. Carl H. Lindner, Jr., Chairman and Chief Executive Officer of the American Financial Group, Cincinnati, OH whose generosity makes the publishing of this book possible.

Cover illustration *"Praying Hands"* by Monicha Love

A Statement From The Author

At age 15, when I was a student at The Old Hopewell Vocational High School in Mississippi, I started writing this book of poems. They were not written because of any special literary skill that I possessed, nor because I had any dream of becoming a writer. They were written to express my burning ambition to go to college and prepare for a better life than could be enjoyed in the rural area where I was born. My first visit to a Doctor took place after I matriculated in College. My tonsils were removed after I entered seminary and this was done in the doctor's office. These things are only mentioned to inform a generation far removed from such unusual conditions.

Writing poetry became an outlet for my emotions and especially my dreams. It served to keep me aspiring for higher attainments as well as improving my ability to think and express myself. These poems are not made available because they are excellent poetry, but to make known to some how faith in God can be consistent and continue through the years. As I read them I find them challenging as well as thought provoking. My first poem is included to give insight into the heart of a teen-ager and to encourage us to have faith in our teen-agers today. My first offering at age 15, is the poem that follows:

I Shall Not Go That Way

I was carried upon a pinnacle
And was shown the beauties of the world,
And its riches which consisted of gold and silver,
And even beautiful girls.
It was the wise old man called Satan
Who carried me on this sight-seeing tour;
He blinded my eyes with great riches
And made me think that it was real and pure.

He bade me compose and sell love songs
That I might acquire a higher education
With greed in my eyes and sin in my heart,
I eagerly grabbed at the chance,
I saw great fame before me,
Much happiness and romance.
Without even thinking of my destiny,
I hurriedly began my task;
I put much of my time to the work
Without a question from a wise person ask.
He made me see as he saw and really think ,
He gave me poison whiskey;
Without I even knowing that I drank;
By my loving money he used his influence
And cast his spell over me;
I could not think wisely and successfully;
I could not think of the right to see
I was groping in darkness and stumbling,
I was about to fall
I could not see a clear pathway in which to walk
Right did not prevail in me at all.
I went on trying to make myself believe
That I was really doing right
I tried to make myself happy;
And did not give my conscience justice;
Morning nor night
But when I had completed my task
And felt that I had done real well;
The simple question most in my mind-
What if this sends my soul to hell?
I began to think and ponder and wonder more seriously;
I began to think how demoralizing my act and its effect
Upon future generations would be;
My eyes began to open and I awoke,
The Lord began to show me the way;
At once I cried out- though I never go to college;
I shall not go that way.

Contents

Preface

The collection of poems in this book spans many years.
I began inspirational writing in the tenth grade. During
my sixty years in ministry I have faced numerous
hardships and experienced the joy of many victories.
These are expressions of my inner-most thoughts and beliefs,
while on this adventure with God. Through prayer, I was able
to persevere and weather the storms of life. There is power in
prayer to change, strengthen and sustain you. So, no matter
what the situation may be, keep on praying.

Keep On Praying
When you are angry and afraid
Over some blunder you have made
And life offers you no shade;
Keep on Praying
When you are weary, troubled and blue
Battle fatigued through and through,
And there's nothing you can do;
Keep on Praying
When you are knocked down and defeated
Lost and lonely and depleted,
And it seems life is completed;
Keep on Praying
When you are bewildered and confused
Humiliated and spirit bruised
And your labors are misused;
Keep on Praying
When your nerves and sinews are pained
Heart-sick and energy drained,
And lost fortunes can't be regained;
Keep on Praying
When hopes are almost gone
Spirit lost from hanging on,
And you are hurting to the bone;
Keep on Praying
Somewhere there's a rainbow in the sky
Faith gives one a seeing eye,
Keep your aim and spirit high;
Keep on Praying

Section One

In His Presence

"Thou wilt shew me the path of life:
in thy presence is fullness of joy; at thy
right hand there are pleasures for evermore."

Psalms 16:11

Oh how sweet it is to Commune with the Creator.

"Prayer has a tendency to throw a reflection of light upon our pathway, and changes our lives all together..."

"Therefore I say unto you, what things soever ye desire, when ye pray, believe that ye receive them, and ye shall have them." Mark 11:24

Great Moments With Jesus

Great moments with Jesus
Moments so rich and rare
Great moments with Jesus
Moments of freedom from care.

Great moments with Jesus
Moments of love divine
Great moments with Jesus
Moments where peace is mine.

Great moments with Jesus
Moments of quiet and peace
Great moments with Jesus
Moments of blessed release.

In Faith

In holy faith I walk each day
I cannot see one inch of the way
Thy tender voice doth lead me
So in faith I follow Thee.

I do not see what lies ahead
But yet I follow without dread
There's comfort when I see your light
That shines around me so bright.

I have only to hear thy call
It strengthens me from a fall
With joy my Savior's near I know.
To lead me wherever I go,

When I feel my weakness, then
I look and see my awful sin
O Thou who died on Calvary
O cleanse my soul and set me free.

O yes, in faith I live
And my little service give
I expect no great reward
For in faith I follow the Lord.

Clinging To The Master

I am clinging to the Master Divine
Who controlleth this heart of mine
With His grace and love I gladly talk
And by His side I gently walk.

Tis a sweet communion I love
As I look to the heavens above
And place my hope and trust in Him
Life seems far sweeter in this realm.

Tis a joy only known by the saints
Who daily prays and never faints
And place their hopes above the world
Who march with banners all unfurled.

At the last will sound the cry well done
When the beautiful life crown is won
When our struggles and toils are o'er here
We shall no longer our burdens bear.

I will ever cling to Him
As I travel thro' this realm
He is my hope, my guide and stay
I'll walk by His side all the way.

All My Cares

Father I bring all my cares to Thee
All my sorrows, grief and woe
Asking Thee to pardon me
No other help I know.

I would bow my head and pray
For the comfort of thy love
Crying brighten up my way
And lead me safely home above.

My heart is troubled with many cares
My body often suffers pain
Often I travel in doubt and fear
Feeling that I live in vain.

But to thy promise I gently cling
And bring all my cares to Thee
Oh hear my praises when I sing
And swiftly soothe and comfort me.

List The Call Of The Master

List, to the call of the Master
List,with thy tenderest care
Calling His lambs to His pasture
That they may no longer fear.

His sweet voice soundeth tender
My child humbly surrender
And Thy hunger I will feed.
I will suppy every need.

He now stands. gently beckoning
Sinner why wilt thou delay
Soon you must give a reckoning
Oh, why not come today.

Oh, he will be your helper
If you'll not reject His Iove
He will be your blessed Savior
And carry you home above.

List, to the voice of the master
Pleading so gently today
Calling his sheep to his pasture
Oh come without delay.

A Pastor's Prayer

Lord, help us build a Church
  Where forgiveness and love abide,
Lifting up a loving Christ;
  Who suffered, bled and died.

Lord, help us build a Church
  That remains in constant prayer,
Where brother helps his brother;
  In a world of pain and care.

Lord, help us build a Church
  Through faith that looks above,
And with Thy saving grace;
  We are all redeemed thru love.

Lord, help us build a Church
  Where souls are led to Christ,
And fed with his blessed Word;
  Of Calvary's awesome price.

Lord, help us build a Church
  Where the Spirit takes control,
Purging out all sin and strife;
    And the wounded are made whole.

Lord, help us build a Church
  That prays, " Lord Jesus come! "
Help us to bear our cross;
  Until at last we are Home.

A Prayer For The Lonely

Lord, help me when I'm lonely,
  To somehow always know—
That Thou art so very near,
No walls can shut Thee out;
When Thy name is called in prayer.

Lord, help me when I'm lonely,
  To somehow always know—
That Thou dost comfort pain,
And draw us to Thine arms;
Our cries are not in vain.

Lord, help me when I'm lonely,
  To somehow always know—
That Thou dost send Thy peace,
To hearts that trust and wait
Thou makest sorrows cease.

Lord, help me when I'm lonely,
  To somehow always know—
My help is from Thee alone,
When great burdens weigh too great;
Love rolls away the stone.

Lord, help me when I'm lonely,
  To somehow always know—
Thou holdest me by Thy hand,
Though far and near I roam;
In all Thy blessed land.

Lord, help me when I'm lonely,
  To simply trust and pray—
In every storm be still;
Until a blessed change has come;
In keeping with Thy will.

I Need Thee Everywhere!

I need Thy presence with me everywhere
I need Thy presence with me everywhere
That I may press along without fear
I need Thy presence everywhere.

I need Thy guidance with me everywhere
I need Thy guidance with me everywhere
That I may press along without fear
I need Thy guidance everywhere.

I need Thy courage with me everywhere
I need Thy courage with me everywhere
That I may press along without fear
I need Thy courage everywhere.

I need Thy Spirit with me everywhere
I need Thy Spirit with me everywhere
That I may press along without fear
I need Thy Spirit everywhere.

Spiritual Vision

God give me open eyes
To see Thy Holy will.
My heart with strength supply
To climb life's rugged hill.

Father take my life,
Subdue my every desire.
Master supply my heart
With Holy Spirit fire.

Erase all wordly care
From my troubled brow.
Make me kneel in prayer
And seek thy Divine Power.

Let me a solider be
Well armed in the fight.
Make me diligent to see
Like a Watchman in the night

Our Father

L ord we praise Thee in the morning
For Thy blessings through the day
And we thank Thee for the dawning.
Hear us as we humbly pray.

We thank Thee for the rays of sunshine,
That drives the dark clouds away.
We thank Thee for Thy love sublime
Lead us gently thru the day.

Usher in the dawn
Of beautiful morn,
And let my heart awaken

Oh let it Arise
Ascend to the skies
And may all my cares be taken.

Amid the dewy flowers
Sweet joyous and refreshing
We spend the lovely hours
Recounting every blessing

Confession

I'm worried from sinning,
My soul's sick with shame,
My heart is afar from the Lord,
My soul is in sorrow, for I know His name,
But I have not kept His holy word.

I go to Him over and over again—
And He gives me peace in my soul;
I'm longing for grace to keep me from sin,
I want to be happy and whole.

My flesh makes my spirit grow weary and worn
And often the battle give o'er—
I pray that some day all my cares will be gone,
And I shall have peace evermore.

Lead Me On

Take my hands O Lord, show me the way.
Take my hands O Lord, show me the way.
The way is dark and I cannot see.
Take my hands O Lord, show me the way.

I am blind O Lord, show me the way.
I am blind O Lord, show me the way.
The way is dark and I cannot see.
I believe O Lord, show me the way.

Lead me on O Lord, show me the way.
Lead me on O Lord, show me the way.
The way is dark and I cannot see.
Lead me on O Lord, show me the way.

I believe O Lord, show me the way.
I believe O Lord, show me the way.
The way is dark and I cannot see.
I believe O Lord, show me the way.

I will obey O Lord, show me the way.
I will obey O Lord, show me the way.
The way is dark and I cannot see.
I will obey O Lord, show me the way.

A Sunday School Teacher's Prayer

Lord, may I see each little child
As a living growing tender being
Made strong, gracious loving mild,
By the life-giving Word I bring.

Lord, may I see each little child
As a living, tender growing being,
Beset by passions strong and mild
Transformed by wisdom that I bring.

Help me to hold most sacred time
For its the very source of life
Make me to know each word sublime
Will make for peace or bitter strife.

Lord, show to me the place I hold
Is greater far than life to me,
And that the blessed story told
Will last through an eternity.

Grant that each Sunday morn's light
Will mean another soul to gain
A soldier girded for life's fight
To face the sunshine and the rain.

Grant that no dark or cloudy sky
May mar the sunshine in my soul
Help me to be too strong to ever lie
In bed, too late to check my roll.

O may the work that I've begun
When passed on to another's hand
Will pass the test of Thy Well Done
Because it meets the Master's plan.

And when I see the score I've made
Marking the destiny of my fate
May the prize I've sought never fade
Because I've done too little, too late.

A Song of Peace

Sons and daughters of mankind
Whatever thy race my be,
Can sweet communion surely find
By trusting Lord in Thee.

Remove the hatred over the years
That flows within our veins,
And dry the bitter mournful tear
Produced by jealous Cain.

For there is wrong in every heart
And none can live in peace
Until the sin which pulls apart
Shall wane and not increase;

No nation filled with civil strife
Can hope to long survive,
Such cancer eats the human life
And leaves no love alive.

O righteous God, please make us free
Of strife and bitter hate,
Illumine us until we see
The Light that makes us great.

Submission

I wondered far away from the fold
With a selfish desire I sought my goal,
Then came the Master to me one day;
Pleading gently, behold the way.

My heart was moved, I saw anew.
The Master's will my duty to do,
I cast aside my every care;
And now I follow my Savior dear.

I seek His face both night and day,
Praying For guidance along the way.
I'm willing to bear the scorn of man;
My aim, my all to follow God's plan.

If

If I should climb the mountain top,
And view the heavenly skies that are blue,
I shall not fail to look back and say,
I owe my success to you.

But if I should fall to the bottom of the heap,
And my name in the hall of fame fail to keep,
I'll take the whipping, bear all the blame,
For bringing myself to disgrace and shame.

Surrender

O God out of a silent heart we thank Thee
Who makest us to see ourselves when we become
egotistic and self-conceited.
O may we always see our impotence
And have ever present that feeling of insecurity
other than with Thee.

May we in a quiet hour see Thee, O God
That Thou mayest strengthen us
and fit us for Thy service.
May a feeling of humility direct our spirit
and cause us to surrender Lord to Thee.

May above the tumult and earthly cares
we lift our hearts to Thee
Loosed from the bondage of darkened fears,
Our souls become eternally free.

May we awaken from peaceful slumber,
And realize our earthly woes.
Let us in humbleness surrender
Protected from assailing foes.

May we find our daily bread
In Thy never changing Word
Let Thy rising from the dead,
Be the message we have heard

May through Thee our souls take flight,
Far beyond the realms of sin;
In our quest for what is right.
May we surrender as helpless men.

Through It All. . .Keep on Praying

Friend

There is a friend I know
Whoever cares for me
He leads me where I go
I am blind and cannot see.

When I try to feel my way
And my heart is filled with doubt
I can always hear Him say
Trust me, I will lead you out.

Oh, He is a comfort to me
For upon Him I can depend
Though I'm blind and cannot see
He who guides me is a friend.

And tho' I am blind
He is a friend to me
He is ever dear and kind
Oh yes, He walks with me.

Purification

O King, O king, long may Thee reign
And send Thy blessings down,
And may we ever Thy praises sing;
Till we shall wear the crown.

Let not vain riches over throw
Our hearts that is Thine own;
But keep our hearts humble and low
That we may reach Thy throne.

Tho'darkness over shadows us,
Help us to seek Thy light,
Give us a spirit of love and trust;
O set our hearts a-right.

Sometimes our bodies become defiled,
Sometimes we stoop to sin,
O make us pure as a child,
Lord prepare us all within.

Our King

Fair and holy is our King
Throughout ages praises ring.
Men shall bow in every land
And shall rise at His command.

Angels sang His holy birth
Raising hope and joyous mirth
Bringing to the earth a blended peace
Bidding fears and sorrows cease.

Though the ages come and go
None can doubt God loved us so,
For He gave His only Son
That redemption's crown be won.

Mission

Lord help me in this mission.
To do Thy sacred will
To obey the commission,
And my calling to fulfill.

Lord help me to lift all men,
Up to Thy throne of grace
From a life of dreadful sin,
And evil's dark embrace

Help me to look above
The lowly ways of men,
Help me to feel Thy love,
And overcome all sin.

My Soul

My soul shall never find rest
Down in this earthly abode
Till I lay my head upon His breast
And lay down my heavy load.

Trials on earth keep me burdened down
Often in trouble I roam
Soon I shall wear a starry crown
And make heaven my home.

No more my soul will rest in despair
Pain, cares, and sorrows will cease
All will be glorious and fair
And filled with everlasting peace.

No trouble will stir my weary soul
Satan will never more annoy
Over my heart love waves will roll
There will be endless joy.

A Light On My Pathway

Oh He is in my mouth
His praise I gladly sing
Like Him there is no other
He is our blessed King
Upon mount Calvary's cross
He died to save the lost
Jesus is a light on my pathway.

Oh He is in my knees
And helps me to bow and pray
To spread rays of sunshine
Along other travelers way
He is with me everywhere I go
And His blessings ever flow
Jesus is a light on my pathway.

Oh He is in my feet
Through Him I gladly walk
And tell His blessed love
To sinners as I talk
Hoping they will see the light
And do whatever is right
Jesus is a light on my pathway.

Oh Jesus is everywhere
So sweetly He guides me
He gives me blessed life
He makes me happy and free
His light is in my soul
And o'er me love waves roll
Jesus is a light on my pathway.

Jesus is a light on my pathway
And He is always shining every day
He is everywhere I go and all around I see
His blessed light ever shines before me.

I'll Follow Thee Anywhere

I am a wayward pilgrim traveler
Traveling thro' this world of care
If you will lead me loving Jesus
I'll follow Thee anywhere.

I have some kindreds - a loving mother
But they can only help me here
If you will lead me loving Jesus
I'll follow Thee anywhere.

On this journey as I travel
I need Thy blessed leading hand
I'll follow Thee if you will lead me
Into thy Promised Land

I need Thy blessed loving guidance
While traveling thro' this world of care
If you will only lead me Jesus
I'll follow Thee anywhere.

God

We will look up to God
Following where His feet have trod
Mindful of His chastening rod,
As He lifts us from the sod.

He will not leave us alone
He's Almighty on His throne
He Is Daniel's rolling stone,
He will not reject His own.

We will lift our praises high
Far beyond the vaulted sky
Where we'll live and never die,
Ever in His watchful eye.

God the Father and the Son
And the Holy Ghost are one
Together brighter than the Sun,
And their work is never done.

So we'll watch and wait and pray
Till the dawn of a brighter~day
Soon the mist will roll away,
In His presence we will stay.

Oh how sweet to live and trust
One who saves us from the dust
Frees us from our sinful lust,
And our treasures doomed to rust.

I Talked Awhile To God
Last Night

I talked awhile to God last night,
And told Him all my troubles and woes.
I begged Him for a little light
To safely guide me past my foes.

God listening in the darkness dim,
Heard my feeble cries
And as my woes were told to Him
He looked with loving eyes.

It seems I heard God speak to me,
And say, " Be still my little child,"
There is much I have to say to thee,
As you travel the tempest wild.

And then He said in a voice so calm,
If thou would seek me every day
My Spirit would be a healing balm,
My love would drive your darkness away.

Thou art not just who turn from me,
And walk in ways that art thine own,
My grace can never set thee free.
When thou dost choose to walk alone.

I rose in shame to face my past
For God had seen my evil ways;
And yet had saved me from the blast
Of Satan's hot and stormy rays.

Tis good to talk to God at night
No matter how dark the way may be;
From Him you'll get a little light;
To light your path and help you see.

Section Two

Never Alone

"... I will never leave thee, nor forsake thee."

Hebrews 13:5

Never Alone

*(Dedicated to my wife, Georgia, our five
wonderful children and 13 grandchildren)*
        May 22, 1992

It seems only yesterday,
When we together became one,
We hardly knew the words to say;
As we faced our rising sun.

It was God's amazing grace,
He set the time and hour
When we would come face to face;
Through His own Holy power.

In time two became three,
We knew both joy and pain,
But then true love is never free;
And often loss is gain.

Souls that love grow and learn,
Lessons bitter and sweet,
That every road has its turn;
As we tread on youthful feet.

Life has its beauty and surprise,
Our children grew now to five,
We still had our starry eyes;
To trust God and survive.

Now the years have come and gone,
We've seen days bright and blue,
We are two again, but not alone;
For God is with us too.

One thing is sure - God is real
He leads us all the way,
And so to Him we'll ever kneel
Till we reach that perfect day.

We thank God for all the years,
We know they'll soon be gone,
He'll see us through toil and tears;
With Him we are **never alone.**

He leads All The Way

Oh yes, He leads every step of the way
And I shall ever follow Him
His smile turns my night into day
And my pathway never grows dim.

His love like an ocean flows
And my heart never grows cold
With His precious smile that glows
Like a shepherd He leads to the fold.

He is all in all to me
In Him I find real life
With His grace I'm ever made free
For He washes away my strife.

He calms me when I'm wild
And guides my straying feet.
As a mother would her child
He makes my life complete.

In All Thy Ways Acknowledge Him

In all thy ways acknowledge Him ,
Only believe He'll bring it to pass,
Hold to a faith that will not dim;
He's sure as dew is on the grass.

No matter what may be your lot,
Friends may despise your way of life,
There is a God who changeth not;
He'll surely bless amid the strife.

He never slumbers while you grieve,
He never turns from you away,
He only ask that you believe;
And never-never cease to pray.

Lift up your eyes unto the hills,
Above the toils of care and strife,
His love o'er flows and seeks to fill;
Your heart with more abundant life.

Jesus Is My Helper

Troubles' and trials in this land
I sometimes think I cannot stand,
But Jesus, is my helper
But Jesus , is my helper
He will all my sorrows gladly share.

When on this tedious journey I go,
Satan strikes a heavy blow
Life seems heavy and hard to me
When all my friends are forsaking me.

When my head and heart are bending low
I can hardly stand my trouble and woe.
But Jesus who is ever near
Will all my sorrows gladly share.

Christ Needed Everywhere

O Christ, Thou art needed
        everywhere-
Men's soul languish in strife
        and pain,
Where proud hearts bleed because
        of fear;
And lives are wasted by greed
        and gain.
O Christ, Thou art needed
        everywhere-
Children are lean and sick
        and poor,
Where parents wander laden
        with care,
On dusty streets and barren
        shore.
O Christ, Thou art needed
        everywhere-
Hopes of men die with the
        dusty past-
Of vanished glory and bounteous
        fare,
Of crowns that fade and cannot
        last.
O Christ, Thou art needed
        everywhere-
Men worship dying gods
        of flesh-
And waste their lives with
        artless care,
Like water flowing through
        open mesh.

O Christ Thou art needed
      everywhere-
Men suffer heartbreak and
      tragic loss-
Who damn their souls to
      dark despair,
And turn their backs upon
      the rugged cross.

Remember

Remember when your path seems long and dreary,
    Do not get blue-
Remember others have had great struggles
      Just like you-
When the sun shines on your pathway,
      Do not feel big,
Remember others have climbed the mountain,
      Continue to dig.
When you fall down in the valley,
      Do not pout,
Remember others have been down there,
      Try to get out.
When the world is talking about you,
      Do not turn back,
Remember a train reaches its station,
      By staying on the track.
When your way seems dark and cloudy,
      Do not stop
Remember those who would reach perfection,
    Have God as a prop.

O Lord

Help me my burdens bear
Often my strength renew
Help me endure my trials here
Until I am safe with you.
As my journey I pursue
Help me to travel on
Strengthen my faith to keep Thee in view
In spite of piercing thorns.
Often when the way seems dark
Shine on my pathway, Lord
And when I call on Thee, oh hark!
And hear my troubled words.
Give to me Thy loving grace
And all my efforts crown
When I shall look into Thy face
And lay my burdens down.

The Evening

When the shades of night appear
And cold death is creeping on
O Savior, then please draw near
And bear my spirit home.

For this body must return
Again to mother earth
This warrant can no mortal shun
Nor count the days with mirth.

When the end of sorrow comes
And no more will trouble rise
Welcome Savior, to bear me home
Beyond the vaulted skies.

O Savior, my blessed refuge
I cannot span Thy flood
Nor cross over the mighty deluge
Without thy cleansing blood.

The Motorist's Prayer Wheel

The Motorist's Prayer Wheel is intended to serve as a reminder that we are our "brother's keeper." (Gen. 4:9) We owe him our best judgement when we are behind the wheel. Like us, he deserves life, love and prosperity. We can avoid "rage" through goodwill and understanding. None of us can be what we ought to be without constant communion with God. Our Bible tells us: "men ought to pray, and not to faint." (Lk. 18:1)

The Motorist's Prayer

Lord give me love for all I meet
On busy highway, or crowded street,
Help me to strive to end the day;
Trouble free from work or play.

Lord keep me e'er cool and calm
Let grace and mercy be my balm
Please give me wisdom as I drive
In peace and safety may all arrive.

Bear Your Burdens
With A Smile

Bear your burdens with a smile
He is near you all the while
When your pathway grows dreary
And you are downcast and weary
Bear your burdens with a smile.

When on this journey you go
And life seems filled with woe
Remember Jesus is near you all the while
And bear your burdens with a smile.

When your way seems dark as night
He will lead you to the light
For He is near you all the while
Just bear your burdens with a smile.

When your trials seem hard to bear
And it seems there's no friend near
Remember He loves you all the while
So bear your burdens with a smile.

When danger is lurking near
And all around you is fear
Remember He keeps you all the while
Then bear your burdens with a smile.

Through It All. . .Keep on Praying

Help Me, Lord!

What manner of people could become so wild?
And labor so hard to hurt God's child,
Or did nothing matter what Christ had done;
To build a church He could call His own.

We owe you nothing for all the years
You have toiled to make a worthy mark,
We only know that not even your tears;
Can keep us from consigning you to the dark.

Be gone you fool! And don't come back
We never want to hear your voice again,
For all we see in you is black;
As well as ugly and full of sin.

We are God's great people you should know
Without you we can have a better show,
Just watch us as we rise and glow;
And on to heaven we will go.

But, oh, the story does not end
At the place we chose around the bend,
The man is not idle or walking the street;
It seems his work is not complete;

There is a God who rules and reigns above,
With hand of mercy and heart of love
He cares so little about man's way;
He keeps the night and rules the day.

This poor man cried: help me, Lord,
Let me depend upon your Word,
Please cover all my ugly sin
And let new life in me begin.

All Things Are Possible With Thee

All things are possible with Thee
Yes, all things are possible with Thee,
I am coming lone and sad,
Thou hast power to make me glad,
Yes, all things are possible with Thee.

All things are possible with Thee
Yes, all things are possible with Thee,
Look upon my sin-sick soul,
Let Thy Spirit take control,
Yes, all things are possible with Thee.

All things are possible with Thee
Yes, all things are possible with Thee
Lord, I come to Thee so low,
Reeling from old Satan's blow,
Yes, all things are possible with Thee.

All things are possible with Thee
Yes, all things are possible with Thee
Deep within my spirit cries,
Longing for the heavenly skies,
Yes, all things are possible with Thee.

All things are possible with Thee
Yes, all things are possible with Thee
Lord give me faith to believe,
Grace and mercy to receive,
Yes, all things are possible with Thee.

All things are possible with Thee
Yes, all things are possible with Thee,
Hear my broken sin-sick soul,
Yeilded now to be made whole,
Yes, all things are possible with Thee

Help Me, Lord!
I Am Scorned

My enemies are come together,
And their goal is to thrust me down,
They have made a vow to make me;
The biggest fool in town.

Their strategy is to use religious zeal-
A desire for a closer walk with God;
That their children might surv,ive,
While I'm bent beneath the rod.

They seek to deny all that I have done,
And forget the rugged race that I have run.
To overcome their dark and dismal past
For a false glory that will not last

They set the whole town a-fire
With rumors of my evil deeds,
And thus brand me as a liar;
Whose message no one should heed.

They spread thoughout the town
Like locusts in the trees,
Spreading venom as they fly
L ike angels in the breeze.
They 'psyche" themselves day and night
Into a state of rage,
To lock their victim in an air tight cage.

As God's people they became so strange
Acting more like soldiers on a rifle range,
They never made room to forgive,
Or to consider that God wants all to live.

continued

The man they sought so much to hate
Was driven from the Holy Gate,
They remembered nothing he had done;
In Winter's cold or Summer's sun

Get out! We don't want to see you again,
Your life is filthy and full of sin,
We know we are on God's Holy side;
And in *His* love we will abide.

His wife long sick was all alone,
There was no care for what she had done,
Though she was calm, modest and sweet;
They took the shoes right off her feet.

Evening's Call

In the cool of the evening
As I walk along
I can feel His presence
And see my wrong
I need His grace to cleanse me
From my sin
That some day to Heaven
I may ascend

I am a poor sinner
Vile as can be
And I'm fully unworthy
Of His love so free
With love he leads me
Day by day
Well my Savior's leading
Me all the way.

In the cool of the evening
When I am sad
He lifts my heavy burdens
And makes me glad
He whispers now gently
In a sweet voice
Calling weary sinner
Come now, rejoice.

Brighter Home

When You have done your best
　　　Yet trouble overtakes you
Sit down in peace, be at rest
The skies are not always blue.

When your friends don't believe
　　　And never seem to trust you
Never sit down, worry or grieve
Because men are not always true.

Sometimes when faced with scorn
　　And overcome by many trials
Never hate that you were born
The crown comes thro' self denial.

You'll find many who are blind
　　　Their poor souls would have died
But in peril they did find.
The Savior, while being tried.

So hardships too, may prove
　　To be a good stepping stone
If you'll only make a move
Toward that brighter home.

The Light Someday

Sometimes I am burdened in this life
And it seems that I never overcome.
On every hand there is strife,
Still I know Jesus leads me home.

Well it seems my path is filled with trials
And I face them as I travel every day.
I remember my Savior faced denial.
If I follow after Him, I must pay.

He takes me thru the shadows
That I too might know the way.
If He's near it will never matter,
For I know I'll see the light of day.

Man

Unguided by the Savior
He is like a helpless vessel
Drifting over the mighty waters
He will never reach his destiny
Unharmed by the tempter.

Loss

If I can make men see God,
In the simple life that I live,
Til I'm laid beneath the sod,
I've only a little service give.

I should expect no reward,
When I owe Him all my life,
He bore the cross though hard,
To banish my sin and strife.

So in the path of duty I walk,
Living a dear friend to man
In deeds as well as talk,
Doing the best to all I can.

To he who would be my comrade,
I would very gently call
To really enlist and aid,
My brother you owe it all.

No matter how great the deed,
Stop and think of the cross
He filled the world's greatest need,
It shall never suffer loss.

I'm Holding On!

When friends are few
And I'm left alone,
When the morning's dew
Has vanished and gone,
I seek the One
Who is always there,
And go to Him,
In secret prayer.

When friends betray
And truth is denied,
When doubt holds sway
And faith is tried,
It is then His call
Comes from above,
I'm your all and all,
You can trust my love.

When clouds appear
And darken the day,
When faith turns to fear,
And joy flies away,
Then I bow low
On bended knee
He hears my cry
And sets me free.

I'm holding on-
I'm holding on-
I'm holding on-
I'm holding on to the Lord,
He guides my feet.
He holds my hand
I'm trusting Him,
Who helps me stand;
I'm holding on to the Lord,
I'm holding on.

Walk On With God

Walk on with God;
In all your joy and sorrow,
Walk on with God;
Amid your toil and care
He leads the way into a brighter tomorrow,
And answer every brokenhearted prayer.

Walk on with God;
He'll lead you by still waters
Walk on with God in pastures bright and green;
In Him you'll find hope that never falters,
A peace sublime the world has never seen.

Walk on with God;
As you travel o'er life's highway,
He'll wipe away each lonely falling tear;
His light will brighten up your cloudy pathway,
And make your vision ever bright and clear.

Walk on with God ,
O soul so young and tender,
Walk on with God, O heart so brave and true;
Walk on with God- and ne'er to sin surrender,
Walk on with God,
Walk on and He will see you through.

The Savior

Though the night is falling
I shall never fear
For I hear Him calling
Saying I am near.

He is a pleasant companion
I'd follow Him all the way
He has prepared a mansion
Where I shall dwell some day.

In the dark valley of sorrow
Yes, in the valley alone
Looking with faith for tomorrow
To live around His throne.

Talk

Talk should be absent of form,
Filled with spirit and zeal,
With force that'll banish harm;
That hearts of Christians can feel.

Only The Master

Only the Master can heal our diseases,
Only a loving Savior who cares—
Only the Master who knows and sees us;
Can understand the grief that we bear.

Only the Master can keep us from straying
Only a Savior can turn us around—
Only the Master keeps us from dying
And bid us warmly ever draw near,

Only the Master will grant us free grace
Only a Savior will our sin forgive—
Only the Master will show us His face
And lovingly grant us power to live.

Only Jesus is a loving friend indeed.
Only Jesus can supply a sinner's need.
You need never doubt Him,
There's no life without Him:

He's the blessed Savior
And He's all you need.

Follow The Savior

Follow the way of Jesus
And learn of His tender love
How He so safely keeps us
Let us look to heaven above.

There's peace in the Savior
Where all is quiet and still
And we are free from the tempter
Sweetly doing our Master's will.

Let us follow Him by the way
And from His word let's feed
Oh listen to His voice as He says
Come and I will fill your need.

Let us humbly follow Him daily
Yes, follow the Savior so kind
Let us work for Him free and gaily
Because of His love divine.

The Savior will never forsake us
Let us follow where he leads
Someday to heaven He'll take us
And bless our humble deeds.

Something Within
Tells Me To Wait On The Lord

Sometimes weary in despair
Often on my knees in prayer,
Hoping night will pass away;
In the golden rays of day;
Something within...
Tells me to wait on the Lord

When labor seems in vain
And confusion comes to reign
Struggling under a heavy load
Traveling down a lonesome road;
Something within ...
Tells me to wait on the Lord.

Sometimes feeling pushed aside
Crushed beneath my sinful pride,
Bent in body and spirit low
Seeking out a way to go;
Something within...
Tells me to wait on the Lord

Something within- something within
Fills my soul while waves of trouble roll—
Tho' my way grows long and hard
I'll depend upon His word;
Something within ...
Tells me to wait upon the Lord.

Temptation

O Spirit that kept me from denial,
And held me fast amidst the trial
Your place of abode I never knew
Nor did I make a request of you.

O Power that stayed my straying hand,
That bode me in that hour to stand,
And made me never betray my face,
Or fall a victim to disgrace.

O Spirit that made me seek a goal
And kept me when I lost control
And tho' it all a mystery be
It must have been the Christ in me.

Passing

There is a day of sadness
In the life of everyone
There is a day of gladness
When life is filled with sun.

The day of grief is never welcomed
Like the sweet day of joy
But change of life is promised
He can defend or destroy.

Oh, mortals let's remember
God's will must be done
That the life glowing ember
Goes out when life is done.

The Topside Of Adversity

" If thou faint in the day of adversity, thy
strength is small." Proverbs 24:10

There's a topside of adversity
That the trusting soul can find,
In a world of deceit and duplicity;
That overwhelms the feeble mind,
From whence comes this madness-
Engulfing the spirit in sadness;
Making sure our step is slow.

There is a topside of adversity
For all who will make the try
With heart and great tenacity;
And wings poised for the sky,
How can we know sweet victory-
If the help that comes so swiftly
From the realm where faith is found.

There is a topside of adversity;
And we reach it round by round
While the spirits filled with hypocrisy-
Never stand on solid ground-
The way may lead to Gethsemane,
And onward to Calvary's brow;
Sometimes through tears we cannot see,
Our God's Almighty power.

Thank you God for adversity
That makes us sober and still,
And in the midst of life's perplexity
We seek to know God's righteous will;
Sometimes the path seems rugged,
We follow where saints have trod,
With footsteps prayerfully studded
We journey homeward to God.

Section Three

Always Praying

"Pray Without Ceasing"
1 Thessalonians 5:17

Determination

I'll lay my work aside
And follow Him today,
I'll need Him for a guide;
To travel this tedious way.

There are deep rivers wide,
That I must someday cross-
With Him I'll span the tide
And never suffer loss.

He needs my life today—
To go and work for Him,
To seek those gone astray;
And bring them back to Him.

Perseverance

Dig where you are,
There's a gold mine,
Watch your own star
Strive to make it shine.

There's a treasure near,
Seek it with all your heart
Filled with hope and cheer
Never from faith depart.

Look not on the hill
But peer into the valley
Watch closely, better still,
And not to all things rally.

Simple things in life,
Oft'n prove to be great;
Filled with lesser strife,
And there joys await.

Dedicated To My Father
(1936)

Among my meditation,
Or in my deepest solitude,
The highest of all inspiration,
This one I can't elude.

Perpetually I'm impressed
It grows greater with the years,
Over a treasure I've possessed,
The joy of it brings tears.

It represents the very best,
Than can ever enter my life,
A model that has stood the test,
Of foes and unknown strife.

This noble character is a light,
That will lead me forever,
No matter what may be my plight,
From Him I will not sever.

His riches do not consist of gold,
Not even houses, or lands
But to me the fleeting years unfold,
His character noble and grand.

To My Mother.

There is nothing sweeter nor fairer,
O darling mother as you.
When all is filled with care-
You never fail to be true.

Within our moments of sorrow
Your love for us console.
We look for a bright tomorrow;
And smile while ages roll.

Mother we can never fail you
Because of your faith in us-
It refreshes our courage anew;
We live a life of perfect trust.

You strengthen our faith in God,
And draw us closer to Him.
We are happier while we trod;
Within this wicked realm.

O mother, our darling mother
When we are about to fail,
When we would go no further
Your love makes us prevail.

Brothers Joined In Heart

Our toiling hands are brown and white
Our flags may differ too;
But we are brothers joined in heart
Our Father's work to do.

Though tongues are strange, all faces light
To hear that sacred Name,
Who shunned the wrong and chose the right;
Who set us free from shame.

Our souls were once in darkness lost;
The debt we could not pay;
When Jesus came He paid the cost
And cancelled sin away.

Beset by sin and gross disgrace,
We hear the Father's call,
"Go tell to ev'ry tribe and race
That I am Lord of all."

We may be far across the sea,
But we are never alone;
The light of God which shines so free
Will lead us safely on!

Admonition

O think what you mean to others
And say one kind little word.
Give a smile for we all are brothers.
Now speak while you may be heard.

A friendly word and a kindly deed
May mend a heart broken with shame
Spoken to one in the time of need.
There's power in the mention of God's name.

Reach out to the fallen a helping hand.
Touch others by your life.
Go forth to better the land,
Make peace where all is strife.

There is much that you can do,
Whether it's giving or in sharing
Or making the sun shine through
Help carry the cross they're bearing.

By Faith He Speaks Again

(Dedicated to the memory of
Dr. Martin Luther King, Jr.)

Into a world of sin he came,
Born to extol his Savior's name,
Preaching the Gospel without shame,
By faith he speaks again.

Tender and young he felt God's call,
He led his people firm and tall,
His spirit towered over all,
By faith he speaks again.

Love carried him to mountain's height,
Hate tried to dim his freedom's light,
He saw the promised land in sight,
By faith he speaks again.

Now he lives in the hearts of men,
All who with justice seeks to win,
And live triumphant over sin,
By faith he speaks again.

He moved the land in every clime,
He gave to life a new sublime,
He left the world while in his prime,
By faith he speaks again.

Sowing

Today we live,
We often sow,
We gladly give,
To life as we go.

Tomorrow we must reap,
Life's harvest grain,
The results we must keep,
Whether sunshine or rain.

The promise is true,
And forever stands,
That whatever we do
Will again face man.

Sweet Olivet

From the mountain of rugged Calvary
   To the heights of Olivet,
Christ ascended to God in victory,
    After paying our awesome debt.

He calls us to our Calvary
   To taste the bitter gall,
But does not leave us nor forget;
   Without Him we would fall.

He brought us to sweet Olivet
   With strong and loving hand,
His grace kept us as we met
   With trials in the land.

Sweet Olivet is our secret place
   Where faith defies dismay,
And humble hearts receive His grace;
   To seek the upward way.

On hilltop high sweet Olivet
   Holds high the rugged cross,
Compelling us to love and forgive;
   That none may suffer loss.

Sweet Olivet, you bring us peace
   Amid the raging strife,
In fellowship, our sorrows cease;
   Through love we find new life.

At Olivet, we'll watch and wait
   Until we hear His call,
And march into Jerusalem's gate;
   To crown Him Lord of all!

Mother

I saw a picture yesterday,
" Across the miles to Mother"
These words I can never say;
For we are near each other.

To me you are very near,
Though we are miles apart,
It's very simple, Mother Dear;
For you are in my heart.

Time nor fortune can erase-
Joy, laughter, nay a tear
No, never your fond embrace
Of love, my mother dear.

You inspire my sweetest song,
Yes, even my loveliest smile-
May your years be ever long;
And all of them worth-while.

O God

I view the distant scene
Often in wonder I roam
Upon my savior's Proimse I lean
And seek a brighter home.

The way often grows dark
I bow my troubled head
In fear and sorrow I hark
He lifts all fear and dread.

I turn my eyes and look to heaven
And call my Savior's name
Thy will on earth as done in Heaven
O lift my heart from shame!

Oh let me feel Thy blessed care
And taste Thy loving grace
O banish away all my fear
Till I shall see Thy face.

Challenge

Why do I sigh with pain
Over efforts that were vain
This maxim holds true
What is done, we can't undo.

The worst feeling to accompany defeat
Is the spirit , "I'll retreat"
If we'll only fight harder then,
The bet is sure that we'll win.

Failure has never marked defeat,
So indelibly and complete
As the willingness to give down,
Forfeiting all rights to the crown,

One cannot experience a greater thrill
Than after falling, climb the hill,
That once to him seemed too steep
For him to climb out of the deep.

My Father

As he travels up the highway of success,
He tries in every way possible to do his best,
He is worthy to walk on the road he tramples
He is to us one great word - *an example!*

I Cannot Fail

In the race of life as I begin
There are many causes for me to sin
But even when I find I'm scorned
There's joy because I've been re-born.

Many try to make the way so dark,
As I falter, I hear him and hark
I am the way, the truth and the light;
Follow me where there is no night.

Though beset by trial and care,
And my pathway oft is filled with fear,
It may be that I must weep and wail;
But with Him I know I cannot fail.

When from the path of truth I'm led
And my weary soul is filled with dread,
Then to my Savior I quickly go
And He ever keeps me with Him I know.

With the Lord I know I cannot fail,
Tho' sometimes I may weep and wail,
But with Him by my side
I'll rise with the tide
With the Lord I know I cannot fail.

Success
(1936)

Success is mine if I but grasp it
With courage strong ever clasp it,
Be hard the task, if I but will;
Can conquer it and greater still.

Love is mine if I but seek it,
To hold, possess and ever keep it,
Undaunted courage is life's demand
Is quite invincible, yes twill stand.

Others succeed, so why can't I?
Surely it's worth it all to try
If I struggle bravely then;
Truly the victor's crown I'll win.

You, too can make your haven high
The rules are simple if you'll try.
A mountain of faith and courage true;
Can make the darkest sky turn blue.

Faults

Don't let the faults we have
Cause us to separate.
Let us feel each other's care
And our love freely penetrate.

On earth there's none good
But all are sojourning brothers
Let us live as we should
In love with one another.

Let mole hills not become mountains
Nor pin scratches vast trenches.
Let's remember that Holy fountain
That from all thirst quenches.

The high as well as low
All belong to God
No matter where we go,
Other feet have trod.

Let these thoughts approach you
What better am I than they?
If to heaven, we must be true
And travel the holiness way.

May I warn you, dear friend,
As you travel along your way.
To this life there's an end
And an awful judgment day.

Oh The Wonderful
Peace In My Soul

Since I gave to Jesus my heart,
And to heaven I've made a start,
I have within my heart no fear
For I feel that He is near.

It makes me happy to know
That Jesus dwells in my soul.
As on my weary journey I go
It makes me happy, free and whole.

I am happy to serve Him each day
And let my light shine on the way
As I journey heaven-ward bound
And spread His blessed Word around.

Oh the wonderful peace in my soul.
Oh the wonderful peace in my soul.
It makes me happy, free and whole
Oh the wonderful peace in my soul.

I am happy to fight against sin
And to help lift fallen men.
I can hear my Savior's voice from afar
Saying, shine wherever you are.

A Church Spire Speaks

The crowning glory of the church;
I reach for the heavens
To symbolize man's reach for a higher life.
I represent man's hope,
The architect of his dreams.
I call him from the depths,
To climb higher than his reach
Though silent, majestic, lofty and high,
I am a messenger of hope to sinners;
And a preacher to the saints.

I am a Spire.
I proclaim the supremacy of God
Earth is His footstool
And Heaven is His throne.
He must be exalted among the heathen,
He must be exalted in the earth.
I am the symbol of man's communion;
I am his connection with the stars-
When that which is common and low, competes for his
    affection,
I call him once again to a high and holy God.

I am a Spire.
I rest very firmly on God's House.
I am a silent witness that He dwells within-
My ministry is to help man:
I am his guiding light;
I lift his vision high
At the end of a weary day when his spirit is low:
I bid him look up to me - and earth loses her spell;
A new gleam fills his eyes as he fixes his gaze
On a home beyond the skies.
Earth is no longer his magnet;
Once again she becomes his mat.

I am a Spire.
A silent spire,
And yet I speak in a language that is beautiful and
    clear-
The wayside pilgrim who gives me audience is never lonely again.
I belong to the church I adorn-
To give her grace and provide the crowning touch.
I never close.
I never sleep.
I will be here as long as this Temple stands-
And, when time decrees that she must fall,
I shall be the first to announce it.
I shall be the first to come down-
But even then, I shall be declaring man's victory or his
    doom.

I am a Spire.
I am your servant, your minister and your friend.
I invite you to look up and see the majesty and wonder
    of God!

The Spire on the New Zion Baptist Church
(Picture courtesy Cincinnati Post - Times Star.
Photographed by Robert E. Stigers.)

This poem was written when Zion Baptist Church was being built in Avondale.

Talk With Jesus

Oh brother let me tell you what to do,
If you would ever find the light so true-
Just search the blessed Savior's word;
Our Lord is worthy to be heard.

Oh brother when it seems you are alone,
Just claim the blessed Savior as your own;
He will fill your empty heart-
And will never from you part.

With Him your little time is never lost,
But before you follow, count the cost;
Then rush quickly to His side-
And accept Him for your guide.

As you follow, your path won't grow dim,
And what a joy to walk with Him
He will lead you beyond the grave;
For He died your soul to save.

Oh talk with Jesus by the way,
He'll drive the darkness away-
His love will make the darkness bright
And flood your path with blessed light.

You'll See The Beauty Of His Smile

Oh, faithful workers true
He'll give you life anew,
Just work gently on,
Until you reach the throne
You'll see the beauty of His smile.

If you'll praise Him every day
As you travel all the way
You'll see the beauty of His smile
If you'll work here all the while.

The Mightest

From the humble places of earth
Come mighty powers
Often descendants of lowly birth
Soar like great towers.
This is far from being understood
By the masses of races
But search closely you'll find good
Often in low places
And the low, the soil shall till
As history traces.
While our hearts are full of mirth
And as we are able
Think of the greatest on earth
Born in a stable.

"The Schemes of Satan"
Vs. "The Power God"

I have seen Satan wear
    A thousand disguises
And spread venom over truth
    To turn it into lies.

I have seen Satan attack the strong
    And make them weak
And cause good friends
    To refuse to speak.

I have seen Satan twist the youth
    And cripple the strong
And blind the wise
    And crown the wrong.

I have seen Satan discourage saints
    And stop them from praying
Confuse the weak and fearful
    And start them straying.

I have seen Satan smite the proud
    And make them humble
Assault the righteous with fire
    And make them stumble.

I have seen Satan darken
    The world's brightest star
And blot from men's view
    The beautiful heaven afar

But I have seen God rise
    And with a touch of His hand.
Set the world upside right
    And restore the fallen man.

" I Have A Dream "

" I have a dream..."
That one day the great discovery will be made:
that sharing is better than keeping;
That understanding is wiser that surmising; that
Peace is sweeter than war; and love is
more excellent than hate.

That one day oppressed people will learn
that the art of survival is to unite and to
make as their goal the welfare of one another.

That envy, rivalry and competition will be replaced
by admiration, understanding and cooperation.

" I have a dream..."
- that one day we will recognize as our worst
enemies, those enemies within: Jealousy, strife,
greed which lead to distrust and division; and
replace these with love, trust and unity.

" I have a dream..."
That one day all men will make the discovery that love
is the answer— and *faith* is the key to Peace,
Prosperity and Brotherhood.

I Found Jesus

I found you dear Jesus
  A long time ago,

Before I fell into all
This sin and woe

You have never left me
  All alone;

It's not your fault
  I must weep and moan.

Come on Jesus take my heart,
    If you don't help me
I'll be torn apart;
    I need you to help me
So take my hand
Hold me up and help me stand.

Flowers

Where is that lovely flower,
That had begun to bloom?
Shall it with its great power
Suddenly cause my doom?

Where is that flower so new
That was growing in love's bed?
Could it really be true,
That this flower of love is dead?

Where is that lovely flower?
That was blooming in love's garden,
To that beautiful flower
I must ask a sincere pardon.

I drink to your sweet virtue
With it's essence so pure.
The quality of your beauty,
Should all true men allure.

Youth

If nature could recall,
Innocent days of youth,
The scars of age could fall
And lies all become truth.

All mortals would return
Without reluctance or dread
Cheeks would again burn,
With a smile that was dead.

The sons of men would shout,
With cries of perfect joy,
Aged ones would jump about
Once more a girl, and boy.

All envy would move,
Off the face of this earth
The hearts that had been famished,
Again be filled with mirth.

Why should nature recall
The sweet bloom of youth?
We can bring about it all,
With love and desire for truth.

Desperate

Feeling weary and dejected
Living in difficult days
Happiness almost unexpected
Leaving My mind in a haze.

My path before me is dark
In sorrow and dread I sit
Almost in agony I hark
Crying for weariness to flit.

Seeing not even a ray of light
Shining on my dreary way
Shining on my conscience bright
Nothing to cheer me day after day.

The world in wonder looks
Seeking a reason for my plight
Seemingly progressive in books
And success, sure as day and night.

Oh! Looking only at the exterior
How could they even suspect
The same as looking at a mirror
Not knowing why it reflects.

Continue

The trouble lies completely hidden
From even an optimist view
Leaving my mind bedridden
But let me tell it to you.

Like an isolated lover
Longing for sweet romance
My case, I want to go to college
And don't have any finance.

The Way To Glory

There's just one way that leads to glory
I shall travel that narrow way;
There's just one way that leads to glory
I shall travel that narrow way.

The way was made by my Savior
I shall travel that narrow way;
That I might live to gain His favor
I shall travel that narrow way.

The Great Call

I heard the Savior in heaven
  Kindly calling today;
Calling His weary children,
  Saying , arise and away.

Away to the field of labor,
  There's plenty of work to do
Go seek the weary sinner;
  Tell of His love so true.

Do not longer sit idle,
  While the moments roll away;
But now your spirits unbridle,
  And carry the message today.

Now heed the Savior's warning,
  Before it is too late—
Go work while it is morning;
  So you may enter the gate.

The Savior calls from heaven,
  Calling now today—
O ye weary children;
  Seek those who have gone astray.

Thou Hast Made Away

Oh we should stop awhile
And lean upon His arm-
We should always smile,
Smile even in the storm.

When our way was dreary,
And we could never see;
Thou Prince of life was near,
To set the captive free.

Because Thou hast made a way,
Yes, Thou blessed prince of life
Thou hast made a way.

When we were lost in sin,
And we were far away
Thou wast our closest friend,
We never more should stray.

When at the dreadful end,
Of this life we come—
We feel Thou art our friend,
And will make us welcome home.

Give Me The Power

Give me the power
　　To steal away
　　To steal away,
　　To steal away,
Give me the power-
　　To watch and pray
　　To watch and pray,
　　To watch and pray,
Give me the power-
　　To watch and pray
When satan tries to get me down

Give me the power
　　To show my love
　　To show my love,
　　To show my love,
Give me the power
　　To show my love
　　To show my love,
　　To show my love,
Give me the power
　　To show my love
When hate sets my soul on fire.

Give me the power
　　To praise the Lord
　　To praise the Lord,
　　To praise the Lord,
Give me the power
　　To praise the Lord
When He turns my night to day.

Meditations On Time

Time marks:

> The passing of the years
> The pain of silent tears
> The footsteps gone astray,
> The light that leads the way.
>
> A love gone amiss,
> The joy of secret bliss,
> The music of the streams
> The fading of life's dreams.

Time shapes:

> The destiny of man,
> Fulfilling of God's plan
> The longing of desire,
> The heart aglow with fire,

Time rewards:

> The quiet enduring love
> The affection born above
> The hope that never cries
> The faith that never dies.

"Keep The Bible Before You"
Dedicated to the American Bible Society

Take hold of your Bible—
And read it with care—
Its message will keep you,
From doubt and despair;
When troubles surround you,
Hiding the sunlight from view,
Hold firm to its promise—
It will surely come true.

Keep the Bible before you—
Let its message implore you,
Let it ever restore you,
And carry you through.

Read of a great Saviour—
Who reigneth above—
Read of His great favour,
And wonderful love—
It tells of His mercy,
And what He will do—
Just how He will help you
And carry you through.

Rely on the Bible—
It will comfort and guide—
Thru life's greatest trial—
Trust nothing beside—
It will keep you contented,
Ever faithful and true
Trust its message and power,
It will carry you through.

The Right Attitude

I will do what I can for you dear Lord,
I will work for you each day:
I will scatter rays of sunshine and love,
Along every travelers way.

Father And Son
Walking Hand In Hand

When he was a child
He saw him as a hero,
A great and noble man-
Who was honest and real
Who did not lie nor steal.

But when the years passed on
He observed his every fault,
And took stock of every wrong-
So he began to leave him alone.

What an awful plight for a Dad
Who finds it hard to confess,
But instead becomes very sad-
That life is such a mess.

Every man makes some mistakes
There was never a perfect man,
Tis no reason to fail his son-
And not try walking hand in hand.

Some strive for great affluence
Thinking all will be well,
There's no substitute for congruence-
Where love and peace can dwell.

The best picture artist can paint
Whether rich, or poor the man,
Is a man holding on to his son-
As they walk hand in hand.

Such a man has mighty power
Though he may be aged and poor,
An Angel will attend him-
As he walks in and out his door.

He is the man that others will envy
But he causes the world to stand,
Because he sticks with his son-
And keeps walking hand in hand.

He Will Make A Way For You

When you are in trouble
And feel you are treated wrong
Just go on and do your best,
And try to move along;
For Jesus is always near
And you need not ever fear,
For He will make a way for you.

No matter if you are in the right
Yet sorrow is your plight
Never give up and sink in despair,
On land or on the sea;
Just bow down on your knee
And he will hear your prayer.

If you have been forsaken
And driven from your home,
Remember that King Jesus
Will gladly help you along;
Your prayers He'll gladly hear
And you need not ever fear,
For He will make a way for you.

Continue

If your head is bowed in sorrow,
And your eyes are blinded with tears
King Jesus is a friend in trouble
He will drive away your fears
Just carry your burdens to Him
While in this troublesome realm;
And He will make a way for you.

At the lonely end of your journey,
And you are weary with life
He will remember your struggles
And will give you eternal life;
He will never leave you then
For it will be a perfect end,
And He will make a way for you.

And He will make a way for you
In spite of what others may do,
Though enemies assail
His power never fails;
And He will make a way for you.

My Servant, Well Done

There awaits a task, a noble task for me to do,
There awaits a chance, a chance to show my colors true
I must be up and doing, doing my very best;
I must ever struggle to pass this awful test,
I have a Savior who will help me when I'm tried,
He will safely lead me over the hill and mountain side.

I have some souls to lift, to lift from the mire,
I have some hearts to kindle, with the gospel fire;
First I must seek the Savior to set my heart a-right
Then I must gladly labor, labor hard until the night.

So when my work is over and I face the setting sun,
He will crown my labor with my Servant, well done.

I must labor in the morning, evening and the night,
I must labor to help and set the hearts of men a-right.
Then when my work is over and I face the setting sun;
He will pass the blessed sentence, My Servant, "Well Done."

Section Four

Quotable Sayings . . .
Words of Wisdom

*"If any of you lack wisdom, let
him ask of God, that giveth to all
men liberally, and upbraideth not;
and it shall be given him."*

James 1:5

The Author's Creed

I have within me an inspiration
I carry with me a determination
I'm striving to get an education
To reach a safe destination.

Reflections On Success

An example should be given in every act of life.

Happy is he who does his best in his day.

Many would like to have good and great fame,
but few are willing to live up to its name.

Many would like to ride the train,
but few are willing to pay the price.

Around the curve of failure lies success.

Failure is the starting point toward the goal of success.

The only hope of one's success depends upon his courage.

The person who lives without a set goal very seldom succeeds.

Every man smiles when he succeeds,
but the strong man smiles in the midst of failure.

Faithfulness and patience are the mother of success.

The success of any person depends upon his ability
to face failures with steadfastness, and courage.

$\mathcal{A}$ word of advice to young people...
Create within you an inspiration
Carry with it determination
Strive to get an education
Success will be your destination.

Happiness, Knowledge and self-control

Happiness has its course to take before reaching us.

No man knows what joy is until he has experienced great sorrow.

The greatest task that a man can accomplish is self-control.

A man sometimes fails to value that which he has,
looking at that he doesn't have.

Knowing why how, where and when to do a thing
is just as essential as doing it.

Strive to let your conduct to be better than your looks.

Real knowledge is that of creativeness from a deep
spiritual soul.

Whoever is honored is criticized. Whoever is loved is hated.
But, it is only he who has never climbed that has never fallen.

Happiness is a hidden treasure, joy must be found. It is not
on the earth, nor in the sea; nor up in the sky,
nor under the ground. It can only be located in the human
heart and mind.

The deepest treasure of great value that lies
buried in the human mind is self-control.

Wise Observations...

Speak and not heard, heard but not listened to,
is the penalty of the loss influence.

If the world was without children, it would be as a
howling desert, and a sea of madness.

It will be known if you are false
It will be known if you are real
The very best thing for one to do
Is to be fair in every deal.

It is well to remember as we onward go
That we shall reap whatever we sow
Which is one obstacle we can't move
No matter how hard we push and shove.

I'd rather die working to build a higher standard
for my race, than to die of my own sinful pleasure
in shame and disgrace.

The person who learns to think for himself finds little to regret.

The ability to discern right from wrong
is something worth striving for.

The pleasure that is often cherished in youth
is regretted in old age.

He that works for honor seldom gets it.

Ignorance of humanity will cause one
to fail to accomplish his aim.

The possibilities of a diligent youth is unlimited.

Life gives the fairest test, and no real scholar will complain.

There is no sure safety for the rider
when riding a mule with his head down.

The world often estimates a man's chance
far greater than he does.

If for right, to lose the world and its favor, means
an inestimable gain.

I'd rather face the condemnation of man most severely,
and feel the smiles of God.

Music has a tendency to cause me to forget
all worldly troubles, and awake an inner spirit that
deeply inspires the soul.

Remember, man, only that his failures
may be a means through which you can profit.

Little wisdom is in a man's heart who has accepted
the world as a substitute for God.

He who wishes to succeed must be willing to master
the situation.

While you have beauty, nourish it
While you have knowledge, add more to it,
While you have strength, strive to keep it,
Whatsoever you sow you must reap.

Love has caused many to run from life
and rush madly into death.

Every failure or success accounts an experience
upon the pages of my book of life.

A leader has two voices to contend with, the
voice of the people, and the voice of God;
the wise submits to the latter.
Whenever the mind conceives a good idea,
execute it immediately.

To be a great man tomorrow, one must
show evidence today.

He who tries unceasingly shall win.
The greatest knowledge one can possess is
knowledge of one's-self, not of the world.

Fourteen "Be's" Of Good Character.

Be: Ambitious   Friendly
        Attentive   Honest
        Brave   Loyal
        Cheerful   Prayerful
        Courageous   Righteous
        Courteous   Trustworthy
        Faithful   Truthful

Everyone has a duty in life to perform,
and happy is he who does his best in his day.

What Does It Mean To Trust Jesus?

To have a spirit of:
Love, forgetfulness, humbleness and helplessness.
Unselfishness, holiness, forgiveness, and righteousness;
Happiness and praise.

To accept a:
Guide and Savior

To have a new:
Thought, song, and prayer
Mind, heart and hope.
Determination and life.

To possess a spirit of:
Rejoicing, gladness and everlasting peace.

Trust Him! Through It All ...
Keep On Praying

To order additional copies of *Through It All...*
Keep On Praying, please send a check or money order
in U.S. funds in the amount of $9.99 plus
shipping and handling to:

Dr. L. Venchael Booth

Shipping and handling charges are as follows:
1-3 books, $2.00, 4-7 books $3.50, 8-10 books $4.00.
For an order of more than 10 books request
discount rate.